W9-BSC-024

DATE DUE

	12/20/05		
	3/10/05		
6			
16	2-18 or 6		
2/4	4/5 or 7		
8/28			
10/18			
9/22/09			

3002

Leder, Jane

Gymnastics

• LEARNING HOW •
Gymnastics

BY
JANE MERSKY LEDER

Bancroft-Sage Publishing

601 Elkcam Circle, Suite C-7, P. O. 355   Marco, Florida 33969-0355 USA

• LEARNING HOW •

Gymnastics

AUTHOR
JANE MERSKY LEDER

EDITED BY
JODY JAMES

DESIGNED BY
CONCEPT and DESIGN

PHOTO CREDITS
Alan Leder: Cover, Pages 5, 10b, 11, 12, 13, 17, 19, 20, 21, 22, 23, 26, 27, 28, 29, 30, 31, 32, 33, 35, 37, 38, 39, 40, 42.
Bettmann Archive: Page 7a.
Wide World Photos: Pages 7b, 9, 16, 48.
Unicorn Photos: Tom McCarthy - Page 10a;
DeGeare - Page 14;
Martin R. Jones - Page 41.

ACKNOWLEDGMENTS
This book is dedicated to all the wonderful people at Lake Shore Academy of Artistic Gymnastics in Chicago, Illinois, for their expertise, cooperation, and patience. Many thanks to David Roth, John Hill, Rory, Jason, Jamie, Sara, Tina, Elizabeth, Charlie F., Charlie T., Suzanne, and Jillian. We couldn't have done this book without you!

TABLE OF CONTENTS

**LIBRARY OF CONGRESS
CATALOGING-IN-PUBLICATION DATA**

Leder, Jane Mersky.
   Learning how: gymnastics / by Jane Mersky Leder; edited by Jody James; illustrated by Concept and Design.
     p.   cm. – (Learning how sports)
   Summary: Discusses getting started in gymnastics, safety, clothing, equipment, and the various moves in competitive and artistic gymnastics.
   ISBN 0-944280-35-8 (lib. bdg.) – ISBN 0-944280-40-4 (pbk.)
   1. Gymnastics – Juvenile literature. [1. Gymnastics.] I. Title. II. Series
GV461.L34   1992
796.44–dc20

    91-23653
    CIP
    AC

**International Standard
Book Number:**
Library Binding 0-944280-35-8
Paperback Binding 0-944280-40-4

**Library of Congress
Catalog Card Number:**
91-23653

INTRODUCTION

The gymnast stands poised on the balance beam. She raises one leg behind her to create a split position called an **arabesque**. Her arms, her body, and her free leg make an artistic line.

The gymnast moves so easily. It is as if she is performing on a floor that is 40 feet wide, instead of on a strip of wood that is only 4 inches wide.

The audience holds its breath as the gymnast does a cartwheel and a back handspring. How does she keep her balance? How can she perform such difficult moves in front of so many people?

The routine is almost over. The gymnast has performed for more than a minute. She has covered the entire length of the balance beam.

Now it is time for her dismount. A *dismount* is a move to get off the balance beam and end the exercise. The gymnast places her hands on the beam. As she flips over, she lands with both feet on the beam at the same time. She is now facing the opposite direction. The gymnast does a somersault off of the beam. She lands with both feet squarely on the mat. The crowd begins to cheer. They have watched a splendid display of skill and concentration.

Many of the young people in the audience are excited. Watching a great gymnast at work has sparked their interest in learning gymnastics.

Whether they will someday compete against other rising stars remains to be seen. For now, the thrill of learning gymnastics is enough.

A good gymnast displays skill and concentration.

CHAPTER ONE:

The History of Gymnastics

Gymnastics was formed early in the nineteenth century. At that time, people had two widely different ideas of what gymnastics should be. One group was led by Friedrich Jahn in Prussia. He saw gymnastics as a body-building sport made up of exercises on equipment. He taught on parallel bars and on the high bar. The other group was led by Pehr Henrik Ling in Sweden. He saw gymnastics as a school fitness activity that did not need equipment.

The two ideas of what the sport should be caused a lot of debate. Even today, there are people who argue about which kind of gymnastics should be taught. Most gymnastics instructors now use some kind of equipment.

Gymnastics was one of the nine sports originally included in the modern Olympics. The first modern Olympics took place in Athens, Greece, in 1896. Seventy-five gymnasts from five countries competed that year. All of the gymnasts were men. Women were not allowed to compete at the Olympics until 1928.

In 1952, individual gymnastic competitions for women were held at the Olympics for the first time. Women from the Soviet Union, led by Larissa Latynina, took over as world leaders in gymnastics.

In the 1970s, two women were responsible for making gymnastics the popular sport it is today. The first was a young Russian girl by the name of Olga Korbut. She was never an Olympic champion. However, her imagination and cute routines made her, and gymnastics, very popular.

Then came Nadia Comaneci from Romania. She was the first gymnast ever to be awarded a perfect score in the Olympic games. Before she and Korbut caught the public's attention, about 7,000 American gymnasts competed once or twice each year. Today, more than 58,000 American athletes participate in competitive gymnastics programs. Women gymnasts now outnumber men gymnasts 7 to 1. An estimated 3.5 million children participate in gymnastics every day!

It wasn't until 1928 that women were allowed to compete at the Olympics.

Olga Korbut, in the 1970s, helped make gymnastics the popular sport that it is today.

Becoming a Gymnast

What does it take to become a gymnast? Most people agree that it takes imagination, hard work, and persistence. *Persistence* means continuing to try, even when you fail.

Every gymnast starts out as a beginner. Every gymnast has fallen out of handstands or tumbled trying to do a cartwheel. The key is to get up and try again.

American gymnast Mary Lou Retton is one of the best-loved gymnasts in the world. In the 1984 Olympics, she won the all-around Gold Medal, the Silver Medal on the vault, and the Bronze Medal on the uneven parallel bars. Mary Lou no longer competes in gymnastics, but she continues to play an active role in the sport.

One of the things she does is answer questions in a magazine called *USA Gymnastics*. Gymnasts write to her in care of the magazine and ask her all kinds of questions. One young gymnast wrote to ask whether Mary Lou ever got really frustrated during practice. She wanted to know what Mary Lou did when that happened. Mary Lou wrote the following:

Yes, I got very frustrated during practice. Every gymnast, at one time or another, gets frustrated. When I would get upset and aggravated, I would talk to myself and calm myself down. I'd say, 'Mary Lou, just calm down and think about what you're doing. You can do this. Really concentrate.' And believe me, this worked for me. Try it!

Mary Lou showed persistence. Even when she was frustrated, she never gave up.

Hard work, imagination, persistence—these are what it takes to be a great gymnast.

American gymnast Mary Lou Retton won a gold medal at the 1984 Olympics.

CHAPTER TWO:

Getting Started

To get started in gymnastics, find a good instructor. Getting proper instruction as a beginner is the key. If you learn the right way to do things from the start, you will become a better gymnast.

Look in the yellow pages of your telephone book under "gymnastics schools" or "gymnastics instruction." If you do not find schools or clubs listed in the yellow pages, check your nearest Parks and Recreation Department or the nearest YMCA or YWCA. If you have a friend who is in gymnastics, ask him or her about it.

This youngster is getting instruction on the balance beam.

Instructor in this photo is helping with a handstand.

However you find a program, you should visit the facility with your parents. Watch a class for gymnasts your age. If the club has a competitive program, watch a team work out. Get as much information as you can. Then talk it over with your parents. Talk about the costs and what your family can afford. Is gymnastics the right sport for you? If so, then get started!

Safety

The gymnastics program you choose should stress safety first. Gymnastics should be done only in a safe place with qualified instructors.

Observe whether the instructors stress safety and good technique. Make sure that the facility is neat and organized. Proper organization and equipment increase the safety of the gymnasts working in the facility. Make certain that there are plenty of mats. The mats should be in good condition.

Before starting a gymnastics program, make sure the instructors are qualified.

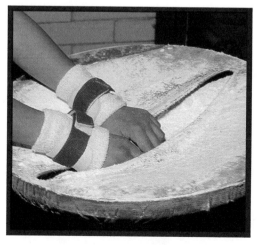

Rosin is used on the hands so that gymnasts will not slip or lose their grip.

Clothing and Equipment

You need very little personal equipment to get started. Girls need a one-piece garment called a *leotard*. Boys need gym shorts, white socks, and a t-shirt.

As you spend more time in a gymnastics program, you will need other clothing and equipment. You will need **grips**, **gloves** (to be worn under grips), wristbands, and gymnastics shoes to start. The clothing is sold at many department stores. You can buy the more specialized equipment at gymnastics clubs or through advertisements in sports magazines. A recent issue of *USA Gymnastics* had five different advertisements for gymnastics equipment.

Girls wear a one-piece leotard and boys wear gym shorts, white socks, and a t-shirt.

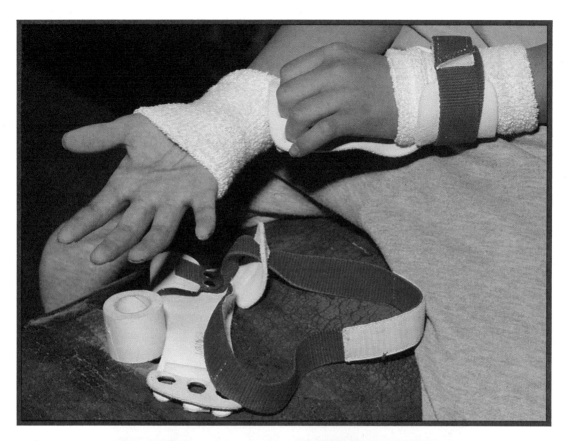

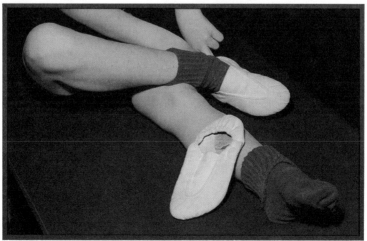

As you spend more time in your gymnastics classes, wrist-bands and gymnastics shoes become part of the clothing required.

CHAPTER THREE:

Branches of Competitive Gymnastics

There are three branches of competitive gymnastics—artistic, rhythmic, and sports acrobatics. Men and women compete separately in all of the branches except sports acrobatics. Sports acrobatics is the newest branch of gymnastic competition.

This gymnast is performing on the balance beam, which is part of the artistic branch of competitive gymnastics.

Artistic Gymnastics

You are probably familiar with artistic gymnastics events. You may not realize, however, that some events are for men only. Others are for women only, and still others are for both men and women. Table 1 shows the events in artistic gymnastics.

Table 1: Artistic Gymnastics Events

Event	Men	Women
Floor Exercises	X	X
Vault	X	X
Pommel Horse	X	
Rings	X	
Parallel Bars	X	
Horizontal Bar	X	
Balance Beam		X
Uneven Bars		X

Floor Exercises

The floor surface used in the floor exercises is 40 feet long and 40 feet wide. It is made of sheets of plywood covered with rubber, foam, or springs. The floor is then topped with a soft elastic material and covered with carpet.

Women do floor exercises to music. Their routines last between 70 and 90 seconds. Most routines include leaps, turns, cartwheels, flips, and other movements. The gymnast must use the whole floor during the routine.

The best women gymnasts in the floor exercises move like graceful dancers. Each move flows freely into the next. The leaps cover a lot of distance. The turns and flips add excitement to the routine.

Men do not work to music. Their routines last from 50 to 70 seconds. They must show a **tumbling series** of great difficulty. Men must have good balance and strength moves. Strength has to be shown with ease.

Gymnast Mary Lou Retton performs in the floor exercises.

Vault

The vaulting horse used in this event is made of wood or a mixture of wood and steel. The horse body is heavily padded. The padding is covered with leather or a material with a non-slip surface. Women vault the width of the vaulting horse. Men use the horse lengthwise.

A **vault** is over in a matter of five or six seconds. The gymnast runs down a runway toward the vaulting horse and jumps off of a springboard. With feet over head, the gymnast lands hands-first on the vaulting horse. Immediately, the gymnast pushes off the vaulting horse. Between the vaulting horse and the floor, the gymnast may do a handspring with twists or a variety of other moves. The height of the vault, the distance the gymnast travels, and the landing are important parts of a good vault.

Both men and women can participate in the vaulting horse event. This vaulting horse is made of wood and heavily padded.

With feet over head, this gymnast lands hands-first on the vaulting horse.

Pommel Horse

The pommel horse is the vaulting horse with the addition of two curved wooden *pommels* (handles) fitted on the top. The pommel horse stands 41 inches from the ground. The pommels can be adjusted from 16 to 17 inches apart.

Many people consider the pommel horse to be the most difficult of all men's gymnastics events. The gymnast performs moves that are different from those in the other men's events. Great arm strength is required, because the gymnast spends most of each routine on only one arm.

The gymnast must balance on one hand while he swings around the pommels, changing movements as he travels along the horse. The only part of the body that should touch the horse are the gymnast's hands.

This gymnast demonstrates a leg swing on the pommel horse.

Rings

The wooden rings are held by straps which are fixed to steel wires. A metal frame holds the wires. The height from the mat surface to the rings is 8 1/2 feet.

The rings event requires great strength. Each routine must include at least two handstands. The gymnast must arrive at one of the handstands through a swing. He must get the other handstand through strength.

At least one position of strength must be held for two seconds. *Holding* means not only keeping the position, but also keeping the rings as still as possible. The rings should not wobble or swing. The gymnast's body should not sag or twist. His arms should not waver or shake.

There is no time limit for a routine on the rings. Most routines though last between 30 and 50 seconds. The best gymnasts may make two or even three somersaults when they dismount.

The "L" position shown here requires great strength.

Parallel Bars

The parallel bars are made of wood and are attached to a metal standing frame. The bars stand six feet above the mat. The parallel bars are for men only.

A routine on the parallel bars is made up of swinging movements above and below the bars. The gymnast passes through **handstands** and shows positions of strength and balance. The gymnast must make at least one swinging move of great difficulty. The gymnast is also required to release and regrasp the bars with both hands during a move of medium or great difficulty. Routines on the parallel bars usually last about 20 seconds, but there is no time limit.

Some of the better gymnasts move outside of the two rails. They perform handstands, **kips** and **hip circles**, among other moves, on only one bar.

The parallel bars event is for men only. The gymnast here demonstrates a shoulder stand.

Horizontal Bar

The horizontal bar, or high bar, is made of steel. The gymnast swings around a single bar that is 8 feet long. The bar stands 8 1/2 feet above the mat. It is 1 1/8 inches in diameter. The bar is supported by steel poles that are held by guy wires for steadiness.

Routines on the horizontal bar last only 15 to 20 seconds, but they are filled with excitement. Routines are done without stopping. The gymnast does a series of swinging moves. He changes his direction and his grip on the bar. The better gymnasts fly over the top of the bar without using their hands.

Many people consider the horizontal bar to be the most exciting of all male gymnastics events. The gymnast never stops as he makes quick changes in body position and grips. During some of these moves, the gymnast cannot see the bar. These moves, called *blind releases*, are very difficult.

Routines on the horizontal bar last only 15 to 20 seconds. The basket swing is part of this gymnast's routine.

Balance Beam

The balance beam is for women only. The beam is made of wood, covered with an elastic pad, and topped with a non-skid material. The wooden beam is 16 feet long and 4 inches wide. It stands 4 feet above the mat.

Just think about it. The gymnast is performing on a strip of wood that is only 4 inches wide. Her job is to make it look as if the beam were 40 feet wide!

Gymnasts learn elements of the balance beam on the floor first. When the gymnast is ready, she begins to work on the balance beam.

A balance beam routine lasts between 70 and 90 seconds. The gymnast must use acrobatic, gymnastic, and dance movements that consist of two or more elements performed in a series.

The best gymnasts change rhythm and level when they perform on the balance beam. They go from sitting on the beam to sailing above it.

The balance beam can be scary at first. It is easy to think you are going to fall. But with practice, the balance beam can become a gymnast's favorite event.

The balance beam is an event for women only. The beam is 16 feet long, but only 4 inches wide.

Uneven Bars

The uneven bars get their name from the fact that one of the two bars is higher than the other. The lower bar is 5 feet above the mat. The upper bar is 8 feet above the mat. Both bars are 8 feet long. The distance between them varies from 30 to 40 inches. Each bar is about 1 1/2 inches in diameter.

A routine on the uneven bars demands strength, concentration, balance, and split-second timing. The gymnast must use both bars. Only four elements in a row can be performed on the same bar. An average time on the uneven bars is 30 seconds.

The uneven bars event is the most thrilling of the women's events. The gymnasts perform big swings that begin in handstands on the high bar. The swings include many hand changes and **pirouettes**.

The front support position is shown here on the uneven bars. The uneven bars event requires strength, concentration, balance, and split-second timing.

Rhythmic Gymnastics

Rhythmic gymnastics became an Olympic sport at the 1984 Olympic Games in Los Angeles, California. Rhythmics are for women only. The gymnasts perform on a 130-foot-square floor area. They work with ropes, hoops, balls, clubs, and ribbons. All of the exercises are performed to music.

The rope is about nine feet long and has no handles. Skills with the rope include skipping, throws, balances, and swings.

The hoop can be made of plastic or wood. It can have round or flat edges. Hoop work includes swinging the hoop, turning it, throwing and catching it, rolling it, and passing one's body through it.

The satin ribbon is attached to a stick. Skills with the ribbon include swings, circles, snaking, spirals, figure eights, and throws.

The two clubs are made of wood or plastic. Skills with the clubs include swings, circles, twirls, throws, and catches.

The moves in rhythmic gymnastics are very graceful. The moves are linked together to make up routines between 60 and 90 seconds long. The moves performed in artistic gymnastics are not allowed in rhythmics.

Sports Acrobatics

Sport acrobatics includes tumbling, pairs, and group exercises. In many ways, sports acrobatics is like the best acrobatics you see at a circus. It became an Olympic sport in 1986.

There are several sections of sports acrobatics. The sections include tumbling for men and women, women's pairs, men's pairs, and mixed pairs. The routines last about 2 1/2 minutes.

Flexibility, strength, and body awareness are important in sports acrobatics. Gymnasts train for sports acrobatics in much the same way they train for artistic gymnastics.

CHAPTER FOUR:

Basic Moves in Artistic Gymnastics

Beginning gymnasts start out slowly. They learn basic moves step by step. Each skill is broken down into small parts. A gymnast must master one part before going on to the next one. This book will describe some of the basic moves in all of the artistic events.

Floor Exercise Skills

The first moves in gymnastics are learned on the floor. There are four basic body positions. In the tuck position, you bring your knees up to your chest. Your body should form a "ball." To do a pike, you bend at the hips and touch the floor with both hands. Be sure to keep your knees straight. To straddle, split your legs out to the side. Keep your body straight and your head in a normal position. In the layout position, you keep your body straight from head to toe, whether you are standing or hanging from a bar or rings.

In the tuck position, you bring your knees up to your chest.

In the pike position, you bend at the hips and touch the floor with both hands.

To straddle, you split your legs to the side. Keep your body straight and your head in a normal position.

In the layout position, your body must be straight from head to toe.

Forward rolls and backward rolls are done in a tuck position. It is important to tuck your chin on your chest and to keep a tight tuck position as you roll. You finish the forward and backward rolls in the squat position with your arms extended over your head.

Have you ever tried to do a handstand or a **headstand**? If so, you know that balancing yourself upside-down requires a lot of concentration. You must form a tight, straight line with your body to keep your balance. When you do a handstand or a headstand, try to hold the position for at least two seconds.

You must be in a tuck position to do both forward and backward rolls.

A handstand requires a great deal of concentration. Your body must form a straight line.

After you have mastered the handstand, you can learn the **cartwheel**. Your approach is the same, but then you turn your hands sideways. Your body makes a quarter turn as you swing and kick to the upside-down position. But you don't stay upside-down like you do in a handstand. You keep going until you are standing up again. Your legs must stay apart to make the action like a rolling wheel as you land one foot after the other.

When performing a cartwheel, your legs must stay apart to make the action appear like a rolling wheel.

Bridging is a skill that you need to learn before you can do more advanced skills. You start by lying on your back on a mat. Keep your heels close to your backside. Put your hands under your shoulders, palms down. Your fingers should point toward your feet.

Now you "bridge up" by pushing down to straighten out your arms and legs. At the same time, lift your hips and arch your body. Place your head between your arms and shift your shoulders over your fingers. Lift one leg straight up facing the ceiling. Then lower that leg and lift the other one.

You must learn how to bridge before you can move to more advanced skills.

If you can do the handstand and the bridge, you are ready to learn a front over, front limber, and back limber. To do a front over, first do a handstand. Keep your head back between your arms. Shift your shoulders backward over your hands. Then arch your feet over to a bridge position on the floor.

To do a front limber, you do a front over. As your feet touch the mat, you move your hips forward over your feet. Then push off your fingertips, with your head between your arms, and stand up with your arms extended over your head.

To do a back limber, you arch backward to a bridge. With your shoulders lifted back over your hands, push off your feet to a handstand. You finish in a standing position with your arms straight up over your head.

After you have learned the handstand and the bridge, you are ready to try a front and back limber.

Basic Vaulting Skills

Young people learning to vault need to master several basic skills. The instructor usually places the horse sideways, approximately chest high to the students.

Running the right way is crucial to good vaulting. You should run on the balls of your feet. Keep your head up and look at the takeoff board and vaulting horse. Keep your arms bent. Pump your arms forward with your legs.

The *hurdle* is a move from the floor to the takeoff board. You keep up your speed as you move onto the board. Take off on the last step of your run. Then bring your feet together and "punch" the board with the balls of both feet.

The action between the board and the vaulting horse is called *preflight*. In preflight, you quickly extend your body forward, reaching with your hands to the vaulting horse.

The approach run is a very important part of the vault.

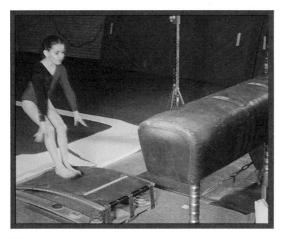

When you move from the floor to the take-off board, it is called the hurdle.

During the preflight, your body is extended forward, reaching with your hands to the vaulting horse.

The next part of a vault is called the *repulsion*. During repulsion, your body should rise and lift off the horse. To do this, your hands must be ahead of your shoulders when you make contact with the horse. Push down hard with your hands, keeping the palms flat and the fingers facing forward.

During the repulsion part of a vault, your body should rise and lift off the horse.

The action between the vaulting horse and the landing is called the *postflight*. To keep your balance when you land, you flex your legs with your feet slightly apart. Bend at the feet, knees, and hips. A good way to practice the landing is to jump off of the vaulting horse onto a landing pad.

Once you have mastered the basic vaulting skills, you will learn a variety of basic vaults. To do a **squat vault**, you go over the horse in a tuck position. To do a **straddle vault**, you pass over the horse in a straddle position, as in a leapfrog action. To do a **stoop vault**, you leave the horse in a pike position.

Basic Pommel Horse Skills

Balance and strength are important in learning pommel horse skills. Beginners practice three different ways of mounting the horse and supporting themselves.

To do the **front support mount**, you jump up and push the pommels down hard. You must keep your arms straight during the mount. The front of your thighs should touch the horse.

The **stride support mount** begins the same way. First you jump to a front support position. Then lift your hips and move one leg between your hands.

To perform a **rear support mount**, you again jump to a front support position. Then tuck your body and move both legs between your hands.

After you learn how to mount the horse, you can try basic moves on the pommel. Your instructor will take you through a series of moves. When you master one, you can go on to the next.

You will learn how to do moves called *swings*. The *scissor swing* is the type most young gymnasts try first. To do the scissor swing, you must open your legs very wide as you swing like a pendulum. You can swing your legs either backward or forward for a scissor swing. You cross your legs over the pommel horse at the end of every swing.

A more advanced move is called **double leg circles**. You must lift each hand from the handles in turn as your legs swing around the pommel horse. Your legs never stop, and they never touch the horse. To do good circles, you must keep your body straight.

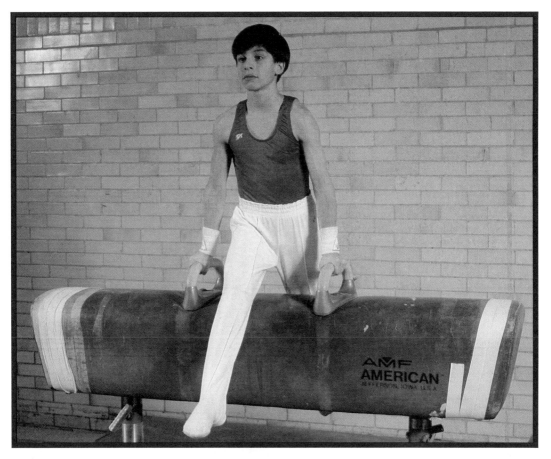

This gymnast shows the stride support mount.

Basic Moves on the Rings

One basic position that most beginners learn to do is the **half lever**. In this position, your arms alone hold you up. You hold your legs straight out in front of you and parallel with the floor. It is important to hold your head up and to keep very still.

Another basic position on the rings is called the **piked inverted hang**. You hang from the rings with your body straight. Then you pike your body and swing your legs forward through your hands. Your arms should be straight.

From this position, you can continue to swing your hips backward and hang for a few seconds. This position is called **skin-the-cat**. Skin-the-cat helps you strengthen your shoulder muscles and increase their flexibility.

There are several other hangs and arm support positions. Your instructor will decide which ones you should learn, and in what order.

Then you will be ready to learn a lift to a **shoulder stand** and eventually a lift to a handstand. To do a shoulder stand, you press your hips upward between the cables and then extend your body. To do a handstand, lift your hips and legs upward until you can push them above your head into a handstand.

This skin-the-cat position helps strengthen your shoulder muscles and increase their flexibility.

Basic Moves on the Parallel Bars

Some of the basic body positions on the parallel bars are like those on the rings. You can support yourself with your arms while keeping your body straight. You can lift your legs, keeping your toes pointed into an "L" position.

You can also support yourself using your upper arms. Your upper arms rest on the bars. Keep the rest of your body tight and straight. From this position, you can swing forward and backward.

Two basic moves from the upper arm swing are called the **front uprise** and the **back uprise**. In the front uprise, you keep your arms straight and move your body into a pike position. In the back uprise, you keep your arms straight and move the rest of your body straight out behind you.

Another way to support yourself on the parallel bars is to hang from a bar with your body in a pike position. As you hang from a bar, you can swing back and forth.

One of the basic body positions on the parallel bars is the straddle "L" position.

Basic Moves on the Horizontal Bar and the Uneven Bars

Many of the moves on the horizontal bar and the uneven bars are the same. There are four basic hand grips on the bar: overgrip, undergrip, mixed grip, and eagle grip. To practice the overgrip, you grab the bar with both palms facing front. To practice the undergrip, both of your palms face back. To practice the mixed grip, one of your palms faces front and the other palm faces back. To practice the eagle grip, you grab the bar behind your head, with both palms facing back. The best way to practice each grip is to hang from the bar, keeping your body in a pike position and your feet a few inches above the mat. From this long-hang position, your instructor will teach you how to use each grip.

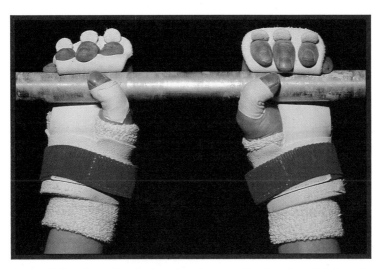

One of the four basic hand grips on the horizontal bar is the overgrip shown above.

Two of the basic mounts for the horizontal bar and the uneven bars are the front support mount and the back pullover mount. In the front support mount, you grip the bar in an overgrip. Keep your arms straight and a shoulder-width apart. Jump up, pushing down on the bar. Your upper thighs should touch the bar. To dismount from this position, bend at the hips and swing your legs forward under the bar. Swing your legs backward, lift the hips, and push down with your arms. Then push the bar away with your hands.

The other way to mount the bar is called the **back pullover mount**. Grip the bar in an overgrip. Then kick one leg forward and upward. Pull your hips with your arms over the bar as you join both legs together. Straighten your arms before you arrive in the front support position.

The back pullover shown by this gymnast is one of the basic mounts for the horizontal bar and the uneven bars.

The Basics on the Balance Beam

Beginners on the balance beam must develop their balancing skills. Most instructors will ask you to practice walking on the beam. Then you practice walking on the beam on your toes. Next, the instructor may tell you to practice side-walking. You stand on your toes and take small steps sideways down the beam.

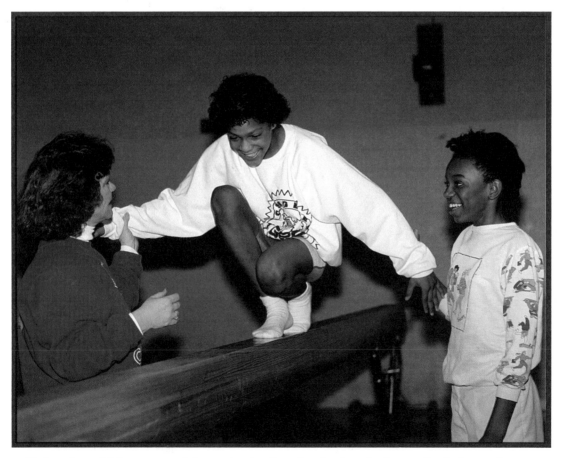

Balancing skills are most important when beginning to learn the balance beam. Practice first with your instructor.

This gymnast demonstrates a balancing skill called develope´.

Another balancing skill is the **developé**. The developé requires that you bring the big toe on one foot to your other knee. Then you extend and straighten your leg without leaning backward or twisting your hips.

There are many different ways to mount the balance beam. You will learn a *front support mount,* **squat mount,** *stride support mount,* and **straddle mount.**

Many of the gymnastics movements on the floor can be done on the balance beam. You can do a forward and backward roll on the beam. Then you will practice doing a cartwheel. You will also practice an arabesque.

Several basic jumps can be used to dismount from the beam. You jump off the side of the beam onto the landing mat. The jumps can be done in a layout, tuck, or straddle position. As you land, keep your balance by flexing your legs with your feet slightly apart. Your feet, knees, and hips should be bent.

CONCLUSION

Gymnastics is exciting and fun. The sport helps you develop key physical skills. It teaches skills—such as confidence and discipline—that can help you in everyday life, too. When you perform a move on gymnastics equipment, you rely on yourself. There is no other team member to whom you can turn. You are in charge!

GLOSSARY

arabesque - a split position in which one leg is raised behind the gymnast, parallel to the floor; creates an artistic line with the arms, body, and free leg

back pullover mount - a way to mount the horizontal or uneven bars; the gymnast uses an overgrip, kicks one leg forward and upward, pulls the hips with the arms over the bar while joining both legs together, and straightens out the arms before arriving in a front support position

back uprise - a move on the parallel bars in which the gymnast swings his body backward, kicks his legs backward through the bottom of the swing, arches his body, and pulls the bar down to arrive at an extended arm support swing

backward roll - a move in which the gymnast lies down, then lifts his or her legs into a pike position, lifts the hips, pushes hard with the arms, and finishes the roll on both knees

cartwheel - a move that begins the same as a handstand; the gymnast turns the hands sideways and makes a quarter turn as he or she swings and kicks the legs to an upside-down position and back around to an upright position

developé - a move in which the gymnast stands on one leg, brings the big toe on the other foot to the knee, and then extends and straightens that leg

double leg circles - an advanced move on the pommel horse in which the gymnast lifts each hand from the handles in turn as his legs swing around and around

forward roll - a move in which the gymnast goes forward onto the right leg, reaches forward and places the hands on the mat or balance beam, extends the left leg upward, lifts the hips, shifts the weight forward, and places the shoulders onto the mat or beam during the roll; the gymnast brings the legs together as he or she pikes the body and then steps out of the roll onto the left foot, then the right foot, as he or she stands

front support mount - a way to mount the pommel horse, uneven bars, horizontal bar, and balance beam

front uprise - a move on the parallel bars; the gymnast swings his body forward, pulls the bars back with his arms, kicks his legs forward, straightens his arms, and extends his body into an arm support swing

gloves - made of sheep leather and treated with lanolin; helps keep the hands soft and can be worn under a grip

grip - a leather strap with holes for two or three fingers; protects the gymnast's palm and provides a better grip

half lever - a basic position on the rings in which the arms hold the gymnast up, with his legs held straight out in front, parallel with the floor

handstand - balancing skill; the gymnast stands on his or her hands with legs extended and the toes pointed

headstand - the gymnast balances on the head with the legs extended and the toes pointed straight up

hip circles - a circle around one of the parallel bars with the gymnast's body revolving around the hips

kips - advanced stunts performed on the parallel bars; stunt begins with a strong back swing; then the gymnast lifts one leg back followed by the other, then glides both legs forward; at the front of the swing, the gymnast arches the back and then brings the legs sharply up toward the bar

piked inverted hang - a basic body position in which the gymnast hangs from the rings with his body straight, pikes his body, and then swings his legs forward through his hands

pirouette - a turn done while the gymnast supports herself on her hands in a handstand

rear support mount - a way to mount the pommel horse

shoulder stand - a position on the rings or parallel bars; the gymnast starts in the "L" position, presses his hips upward, and then extends his body into a shoulder stand

skin-the-cat - a position on the rings that continues from a piked inverted hang; the gymnast continues to swing his hips backward and hangs for a few seconds

squat mount - a way to mount the balance beam; the gymnast jumps up, pushes the beam down, tucks the body, and keeps the hands on the beam as she lands in the squat position

squat vault - going over the vaulting horse in a squat position

stoop vault - to leave the vaulting horse in a pike position

straddle mount - a way to mount the balance beam; the mount is done the same way as the squat mount, except the gymnast pikes the hips and straddles the legs to the side

straddle vault - going over the vaulting horse with the legs straddled in a leapfrog position

stride support mount - a way to mount the pommel horse or the balance beam

tumbling series - a combination of rolling, turning, handsprings, and somersaults with different speeds and twisting variations

vault - one of the eight events in artistic gymnastics